FITTING IN

Monologues for Boys and Girls

Raf Mauro

Dramaline Publications
36-851 Palm View Road
Rancho Mirage, CA 92270
Phone 619/770-6076 Fax 619/770-4507

Cover design, John Sabel

This book is printed on 55# Glatfelter acid-free paper, a paper that meets the requirements of the American Standard of Permanence of paper for printed library material.

CONTENTS

INTRODUCTION

Regarding the "Fitting In" theme of this book: my feelings about this are simply that fitting in is a goal we all share. Just wanting to fit in, to belong, to be accepted, to be recognized, and to be liked are important to everyone. Young or old, I think we're just saying, "Hi, it's me. Wanna like me? I'm not so bad. Want me to like you?" We're all just trying to fit in, right? And sometimes, no matter how hard we try, we just can't, or don't, belong to something. Then, often, suddenly, when we least expect it, acceptance and people who like us are all around.

Sometimes we take the easy and gentle friends for granted. Same for our families, our pets. It's human nature, I guess. When we're growing up, we need to feel like we belong. That's also human nature. So, you hang with the kids that like what you like, and feel like you do.

Acceptance it vitally important. And if you feel accepted in your family first, it's a great start. I hardly ever felt like I was part of my family. They even used to speak their native language when they didn't want me to know what was going on. Talk about feeling like you don't belong. I think, from time to time, we all have those "on the outside looking in" feelings. Even when we're older, we often feel left out and long to be part of things, to fit in and be accepted. And when we *are* accepted, we feel like we can fly.

Through these monologues, I've attempted to capture the importance of being part of things. And most of them—not all, but most—come from real-life experiences. I took a nip here, a tuck there, but most are based on real things that happened to real people. There really is a cousin Artie, and I really acted like a coward over a dog and in front of Mary Frances, and the nuns did some totally weird things to me and others, and I went camping and hiking.

So, allow yourself to explore your own feelings where they connect with the feelings in a monologue. You might recognize yourself or a friend, or you may have had a similar experience. It may not have been an identical experience, but the feelings may be familiar to you.

We've all heard the old sayings: "You've got to be a friend to make a friend" and "Love and friendship, the more you give, the more you *can* give and the more you get." These are good sayings, but sometimes life is more complicated than sayings, and sometimes, as hard as we try, friends are difficult to make. But don't be discouraged, because deep down inside us all is a special friend called *creativity* that can often be the greatest friend of all.

GIRLS:

MARIE

Marie's friend is leaving. Now where does she belong?

Listen to this. This is what I hear every time I call my friend. "Hi, my name is Neesha. You have just reached . . . what? . . . I'm the personal secretary for . . . what? . . . I am Dr. Oldenberry's private secretary, please leave your number, and mess . . . number and your name and a brief message and . . . what? . . . after the tone . . . beep and we'll get back to you . . . when we, as soon as we can. Thank you."

I mean, who is she kidding with this message? It's obvious that her mother is standing right next to her, coaching her and try . . . telling her what to say and everything. Ya know, when . . . I mean, if, when you call a, the . . . my house, my mother just leaves a regular message. Like, ya know, "Hello, thanks for calling. . . ." And she says the number that we are, and then she says, "Please leave a message after the tone." That's it—poom! So, I mean, it's, ya know, my mother's not a doctor like her mother. But, ya know, her mother can't cook like my mother, either.

So, 'cause when she comes over here, we always play together in the backyard and we always have a great time with her dog and my dog because her dog and my dog get along real great.

She's gonna be moving soon. Nobody liked Neesha when she came into the neighborhood, but she's just like everybody else. They think she's different; a brace on your leg doesn't make you different. I mean, she likes the same things I like and we play together and do our homework together all the time.

Ya know, once, when she first moved here, we climbed up her orange tree to get the oranges at the tippity top and it was real scary and we both got up there and ya know what? We couldn't get her down and our dads had to come and get us out of the tree. They had to bring a ladder and they were all laughing and giggling. We didn't think that it was funny so, ya know, we just kinda hugged each other on the branch and waited for them to get us down.

It's true, ya know, what the people in the neighborhood say: "Wherever you see one of us, you see the other one." But Neesha's moving away at the end of the month . . . to a state far away, like Arizona or some stupid state like that, and we . . . we're not going to be able to see each other anymore. I think I'm just gonna die . . . I think I'm just gonna die . . . ya know—poom!

MICHELLE

Michelle and her brother, dancing and basketball: It depends where one fits in.

Well, my brother's really got me . . . ah . . . I don't know, steamed now! Got it?! He's a year younger than me and he thinks he's so much better than I am. Every time we go to watch him play basketball, my mother just raves about what a star he is on the team and "He's the best one! . . ." All because our neighbor from down the block showed him how to shoot a basketball two years ago. So he's ahead of the other kids now because he knows how to do it better. It's not that he brags about it or anything, but he's constantly, well, Mom is, she's constantly saying how neat he is and what a star he is, and everything. And she used to say that about me . . . when I was taking my ballet classes—my dance classes.

I took jazz and ballet. I stopped taking them for a while, after my last recital. I just didn't want to do it for a while. So now she never says anything to me like she does him. And it's not because when I was doing this plie that goes into a pir . . . perro . . . turn, like this (*She demonstrates*) and I fell . . . I didn't fall this time. But I did fall then and my brother and some of his friends laughed. He made Tommy Cassell laugh. Tommy is, was, so cool right up to that time. Now all the girls from class I used to hang around with don't talk to me anymore because I don't go to class with them. They think I'm a snob because I don't go to class with them. They think that I think that I don't want to hang around with them, and I'm too good for them. I still dance. I was in the school play and the man from down the block and his wife came and they said I was a great dancer.

I miss my mom driving me home from class 'cause we used to talk and we'd stop and get snacks in Chinatown. I think I'll go back to class. Dancing is good exercise, and I miss it. Tommy's sister is in the class now.

JENNIFER

The Ghost of Halloween Past: Left out by the Great Pumpkin.

Mrs. O'Flanges was having a Halloween party for her son Petra the Putrid last October. Well actually, last October was just last week . . . and all the kids in the neighborhood were invited to go, and for some reason I wasn't invited. I mean, everyone on my block goes. That's just how it is. If one goes, we all go. We all grew up together. I said to them, "What are you guys doing for Halloween?" They said they were going to go trick-or-treating, and then to the party over at Petra's house. I said, "What party? Can I come?" They said they didn't think I was invited. Then they all, like, started giggling and like shuffling their feet, like, like this (*She shuffles and shifts her feet nervously*) while they were giggling and they punched each other in the arm. "See ya . . . What are you gonna wear?" Ralph Lasserella said. Clark punched him in the arm and said, "Be cool, dude!" And they left. Why wasn't I invited? What the heck did I ever do to Mrs. O'Flanges? I'm usually nice to Putrid.

So, after, when we were trick-or-treating, every apartment said, "Aren't you kids a little old for this?" Like they could tell who we were. Everything was cool until it came time to go to the party. I went home, and my mom asked me if I was going to a party, or something. Going to a party?! Boy, is she something. "No!" I just sit on the stoop and watch the kids, in their costumes still, going into the O'Flanges two buildings down. The music and the noise from the second-floor windows was way loud. I got up and walked down the street to Putrid's building, but like this, like I was a zombie going to my grave. I walked in the building and up the dark stairs to the second floor, very, very slowly, like this, and very quietly. I tried not to make any noise. I could hear the party going on as I creeped up the stairs. Everybody didn't sound like they were having a good time. I could hear Alice's laugh. She has the best laugh. Then I heard old Putrid's voice, and Clark's. I don't know why, but when it got quiet for a second, I said in this like kind of ghost voice, "Ooooooo, Ooooooooooo!" And Mrs. O'Flanges called down, "Who's there? Who's there?" And I said, "Oooooooo, I am The Ghost of Halloween!" Real spooky like, ya' know. "I am The Ghost of Halloween!" She says, "Well come on up, ghost, and join the party." I just turned around and went back down the stairs so fast. I didn't feel like I was really invited. A ghost could go, but not a human being. When I went home, my mother said, "Putrid, er . . . Petra called and wanted to know why you aren't at his party. And he said Ralph was the only one who thought your ghost thing was cool. What ghost thing?" I almost didn't hear her finish. Zoom!

PATRICIA

Patricia and the witch, Halloween, the 'hood, and me.

Like, Halloween in my neighborhood is so way best I can't believe it! It's because all the parents get into it, too. People decorate their houses and lawns and stuff and they get dressed up. This last Halloween, I went over to my friend Kirk's house, and I was a Gypsy. I swirled my skirt around like this (*She swirls*) and I had a black fan.

Kirk's mother was dressed like a real witch. She had a, oh yeah, a big black, pointy hat and black dress kinda thing, and a fake nose, and green stuff on her face. Kirk was dressed like a baseball player that committed suicide. He told me why, something about a baseball strike, I don't remember. His mom had the garage open and decorated all in black, and an eerie green light. She had this big er . . . what do you call it? . . . Oh, a cauld . . . cauld . . . cauldron! Yeah, and she had dry ice in it so it looked like it was smoking, or something.

When people came to the door, the Gypsy, that's me, would greet them. I would say in this foreign kind of accent I made up, "I welcome you to the witch's house. Beware of the dead baseball player. The witch will grant you a wish if you say the right words." The words were trick-or-treat. Then Kirk would get up from the floor, or come from behind the door and try to scare them. But he's a little kid and not too scary. Then his mom would laugh in this high, squeaky

voice, like this (*She laughs*) and it was so cool. One
little girl got so afraid she wouldn't even walk in with
her father, and she started to cry. Kirk's mom took off
her hat and nose and said, "It's okay, sweetie, I'm just
Kirk's mom." She had to do that a bunch of times.

On my way home that night, I was near my house
when a guy dressed up like a Power Ranger jumped
out from behind a tree and scared me. Only for a
second. I mean, a Power Ranger? He must be a real
lame-o.

I love my neighborhood, I feel like I belong here.

DEBBIE

Sometimes it's best if the misfits fit together.

Ya know that feeling you get in the pit of your stomach? Ya know, the feeling you get when they tell you that you have to have braces? I just had to go on my bed and die there when they told me it was final. I told my mom that I like my teeth the way they are. I told the dentist that I like my teeth the way they are, I don't need braces. What's the matter with these people? Every time, they said, "Yes, you do." That's when I get that heart-in-the pit feeling.

So, I go to the dentist. I go, "How about one of those plastic retainer thing-ees you just wear at night?" He goes, "No, no, you'll just forget to do it." How does he know what I'm going to forget? What's he got, some kind of ESP or something? Who does he think he is? Who does he think I am?

Now, I have a Cyclone fence in my mouth and school starts in two days. I can't go back to school. Look at these things. I might as well just die. Dad says it's against the law not to go to school. Stupid law. I know, I'll just find a seat in the back row in the corner and I won't say anything for a year and a half. No, I was right the first time . . . I should just die . . . or hang out with people who have braces.

I can't stand people with braces.

JOANNE

Joanne's life keeps taking new twists and turns. How is she ever going to fit in anywhere?

It's been a long time since Mom and Dad got a divorce. For a long time before the divorce, it was a lot of yelling, slamming doors, and crying, and me and Mom moving. We moved four times. Four new schools, no time to make friends or find out who to hang with and where to go.

But we've been here for almost two years now, and even though Dad lives very far away, he calls me on the phone and we talk and he asks me about school and my hair and junk. Sometimes he sends me videos of him and his work. He's an architect. He tapes the buildings he designs. They're very nice. Not too big.

Yesterday, Mom told me that her and her boyfriend, Sam—he's a big plumber, maybe you saw his commercial "Sam, Sam, The Plumbing Man"—are, well . . . like, going to get married! I'll have two dads, she said. Then she goes, "And you'll have three new sisters, won't that be great?"

Okay, Sam's all right, he's almost cool, and he's around, but the youngest of four girls? This could be a major disaster. Nobody will ever have any time for me, I'll bet. Okay, maybe I'll get to borrow some of their clothes, or they might give me some tips about growing up and acting mature or, maybe, like, I'll get lost in the crowd. I mean, Mom has to be their mother too, right?

How will we all get out of the house on time in the morning? Sam's a plumber—he better have a house with a lot of bathrooms.

Mom, do you know what you're doing? Video tapes may not be enough.

MARRIETTA

Marrietta doesn't realize it, but she really feels like she belongs but ... "Not on Easter!"

Do you like Easter? I'm not crazy about Easter. It's not cool. In fact, of all the holidays, Easter makes the least sense to me. I mean, I understand all the religious stuff about it, and getting a new dress and sometimes a whole new outfit. Like, that's not where my head is at, right? Like in my house, we do Easter egg hunts. We do Easter egg hunts up pretty big. Well, the little kids get some fun out of it. We're up all night, the night before, coloring eggs. You know what that means? First you gotta boil the eggs, and then when they're boiled you gotta take them out of the water very carefully because the shells could crack. You don't want that. You gotta use one of these special take-the-eggs-out-of-the-water things. (*She demonstrates*) Then you wait for them to cool off. While you're waiting, you boil more eggs. Then, when they're cool, that's when it starts in my family. It's a wall of talking: "That's my yellow!" "Mom, he's using my blue!" "Oh, shut up!" "No, you shut up!" "Mom, she told me to shut up!" Then my older sister gets nuts and starts painting little flowers and bunnies on her eggs. "That's nice dear, just lovely." "Hey, how come nobody says my eggs are lovely?" My brother goes, "Because they look like little, dirty pieces of ... " "Arnie, stop picking on your sister.

Let's all show each other a little kindness, please."
We all say we will. We don't much.
The next day, so many people show up it's nuts!
Well, we hide over a hundred eggs. Thing is, Mom
hides them and we have to look like everybody else.
Friends, relatives, people from the 'hood, everybody
is looking. I don't like to feel left out, so I crawl
around like everybody else. (*She demonstrates*) Last
year I almost ruined my Easter dress and shoes and
really cool socks with lace. So, like, who finds the
most wins a prize. I won a chocolate Easter egg. Like
I need another egg. Too many eggs, too many eggs.
Maybe I'm just in a bad mood.

SAMANTHA

Sometimes you just don't know who your real friends are.

The wind blew our sign down again last week. The guys and me, we made a baseball field in the vacant lot next to Mr. Bondi's house. That's how I found out about the field. I was at his house and saw them out the window. He suggested I go and join them. He's also a teacher of mine from school. So, we made this baseball field so we could play ball, and then we put up a sign that said it was our baseball field. We made the sign out of some tin, or something, that big-mouth Kenny Mitchell got. It's better if you don't ask Kenny where he got things. Anyway, the wind kept blowing the sign over. About two or three times a week, over it went. It's very windy on that side of the field. No matter how hard we put the sign up, the wind would blow it over.

I helped a lot, and no matter how much I helped, Kenny would always be there saying how dumb I am and, "Who needs this moike of a girl hanging around?" I don't know what a moike is, but I don't like it. He would call me stupid, and then he would say it's the wind's fault and that it's "the stupid sign's fault. What a stupid sign. It don't even know how to stay up."

So, I was over Mr. Bondi's house, and he was working in his yard on the bushes and flowers and junk, and I asked him about the sign. He said, "Put holes in it. Don't you remember what I taught you about wind resistance at the beginning of the year?" Cool! I did *then*. Then him and me . . . oh, no, that's he and I, went out that night, and while he held the ladder, I climbed up and drilled holes in the sign. It was scary on that ladder because it was so windy. The wind was big-time wind all night. My mom works late, at the restaurant, and Dad lives in San Francisco, so I stay out pretty late. It doesn't do any good because the boys, er dudes, don't let me hang with them. You should've seen me on that ladder. I was going like this and waving back and forth. (*She demonstrates*) I thought I was gonna fall to my death, or hurl.

The next day, when we all went out to the field, everybody saw that the sign was still up. I thought the dudes would like me after that. I was just gonna tell them that I did it when big-mouth Kenny started yelling, "Somebody put holes in our sign! Who's the idiot who put holes in the sign?" I said, "Maybe the wind won't blow it down now." He said, "Get outta here, Samantha! Stupid sign!"

I don't wear my hat like he does anymore, and somebody should tell him that the Grunge Look is dead. How can a sign be stupid? He's stupid. I wish there were some girls in this area.

ARNELLA-JEAN

Parlez-vous ... what?

My parents wanted me to study French. My mom's idea, and my dad shrugged. I was away a long time—in a hospital. When I got out, not many of my old friends were around. My mom thought putting me in a French class would broaden my, what did she call it? "My acquaintance base." Excuse me while I puke. So, I had to go to a special class after school because my school doesn't offer it. So, not only do I not get to hang with the buds I have left, but I'm in a class with a bunch of lame-o little kids and have to learn how to speak French. Not something cool like Italian or Japanese. *Parlez-vous français*? Junk like that. Only thing is, I don't think I can learn this stuff. The thing with French is how you're supposed to say it. You gotta twist your mouth around and you look like a spaz or an alien. And, and when you read it, it's nothing like what it looks like. In French, you either don't pronounce the letters in the front of the word, or the letters in the middle of the word, or the letters at the end of the word. Sometimes you don't pronounce them in combination, and sometimes you don't pronounce any of the letters in the word. What's up with that!? Take *moi* for instance. You only pronounce the "m" like an "m." After that, you're on your own. The word *oui* ["yes," pronounced "we"] is spelled o-u-i. That's not "we" that's "o-oou-i!" The word *vous* has a "s" on the end of it you never use! That's crazy!

There are really only two reasons to stay in the class. Well, three. Mom makes me go, Gina Grace Santapietro, and a nice guy named Brad who likes to play Slap Ball behind the school. The sun shines off his braces when he smiles. So cool.

MIMSY

Here we go again. It's Artie time. He doesn't know how good he has it.

I don't guess anybody's told you about my cousin Artie. We have a big family, lots and lots of cousins. Some of us are around the same age, so we hang. Artie is family, so you got to play with him. That's cool. Families are different than friends. You don't get to pick families. So, I'm home and Artie calls. "Hello?" That's me. "Louie is going crazy! He's throwing things and yellin'! He says he's gonna kill somebody! Maybe me! Help, you gotta do somefin!" That's my cousin Artie talking about his big brother, Louie. Artie talks a little funny.

Artie was a mess. He was carrying on worse than the parrot in Aladdin. He's goin,' "Help me! You gotta do somethin'! He's insane, help, quick!" Then I hear, BOOM! BAM! BANG! CRASH! BAM! Then, a dial tone. I call back; it's busy. I think about who to call, and I call my brother, Freddie. He's way older than I am, and like he's an intern at the hospital, okay? Okay. I tell him what's up, and he says, "Relax, they're just a couple of kids and you're a girl half their size. It's not our business, stay out of it." Like duh, I didn't even think of that. Artie calls. "He's breaking things! Oh my God! He's throwing the phone! Did you get help?" BING! BABOOM! BADABAM! Dial tone. I think, cool, my aunt and uncle are going to go ballistic. Glad I don't belong to that family.

I go watch TV. After a little while, I call just to see. Artie answers. "Sup?" I ask, "What's up over there?" He says he's watching TV and that his brother went to shoot some hoop. That was it! Weird, right? Like, tell me *my* family isn't way better!

LINDA

Sometimes, the best things come from you, and your best friends are right under your nose.

I used to love Mother's Day. I'd get Mom a little gift. Handkerchiefs, candy, or some cologne—something. It was easy, and she liked it. Made a big fuss. Sometimes, she even cried a little. Then, this year, it all changed. She goes to me, she goes. "Make me something. I'd like that a lot, in fact I'd love it if you made me something instead of buying me something."

I don't make things. I play video games, read, get good grades—I don't make things. I was very stuck. Like, like, I'm not a maker. So I tried to think of what I could make for her. Not an ashtray. She doesn't smoke, thank God. An alien spacecraft? No. A belt out of some old piece of leather? I don't think so. I don't knit or sew. I mean, like, I get an allowance. I could buy her something. I don't even have any friends who make things. I hardly know anybody here. It's just me and Mom. She's like my friend, right? So I want to do what she likes. School is no help—I have a tutor because I can't go to school until next September after my lungs heal. I can only do things for a few minutes at a time. I could make her a card. I could write something in it like a poem. That's like making her something. It could go:
"I'm never scared because you are here
You're never alone because I am here

You take good care of me and even when you're
working or busy, I know you love me and will
love me and will stop if it's important . . .
That part doesn't rhyme.
"When I cough and cannot stop
Your hands are cool and the soup is hot and just
ducky
My mom is my best friend, are others this lucky?
Happy Mother's Day."
Hope she likes it better than handkerchiefs.

SHARON

Sometimes, belonging is just trying something new
. . . or new to you.

Think being a clown is easy? Forget it! Think again.
All I wanted to do was be in the school Spring Splash.
Every year, we have this thing, and every year almost
everybody in school gets up and does something.
Either they sing, play an instrument—not too good—
or they build something, or put on little skits.
Everybody except the major dweebs and geeks, or the
people that can't do stuff. I am not a dweeb or geek.
But I never do anything.

So, this year, I ask Shelly, Margi, and Helen if I
could be in their thing. They said they were doing a
circus and that I could be the clown. I said, "Cool,
what do I have to do?" Here's what I wound up doing.
First, I had to put on this wig. (*She puts on a wig.*)
Then I had to paint these big dots on my cheeks. (*She
paints.*) Then I had to chase people around and squirt
them with a water cannon. I could spray anybody I
wanted. All of that was kind of cool, but I was still
wondering if it was for me. I figured, like, it doesn't
hurt, so, okay. When we practiced—rehearsal, they
called it—I always had to carry all their junk and
stuff. They said it was because I was new. I mean,
like, chairs for balancing and balls for juggling and
stuff. Then just before we were going to go on, Helen
hands me a big, whipped-cream pie. I said, "What's
up with this?" We didn't prac . . . rehearse it. Helen

goes, "When Shelly or Margi pull on their ear, you hit the Assistant Principal, Mrs. Birch, in the face with the pie. That will be *so* cool." I was very excited about that. So, I went out and sprayed people, I rolled on the floor, and begged like a dog, like this. (*She demonstrates.*) Then, near the end, I see Shelly tug on her ear. I move over to where Mrs. Birch is sitting, and I was just about to hit her with the pie when she reached out and pushed it into my face! The audience went wild! I thought they were all gonna lose it! It was so great. The best time of my entire life.

Clowning is not easy, but it's way fun.

PHYLLIS

Being the most popular girl in school is a good thing, unless it really hurts.

Lorraine Cobb is the most pretty and coolest girl in my class. The most popular, and she gets like *a's* on everything. I always wished I could be like her. Then, one day, we're in class and the teacher, Sister Beat-You-Till-You-Bleed, went out of the room and Frank Stavola was the monitor. What a joke. Like, he's the worst one of all the boys. He says mean things to kids while his dudes are hanging around, and, naturally, they all laugh. He thinks he's such a big man. Major jerk, hamster cheeks, geek-o-rama!   Nun-the-Terrible was gone for just a second when he started picking on Lorraine. He goes, "Hey, brainiac, who planted your hair?" And a lot of other really gross and stupid stuff. His dudes are giggling, and even some of the girls, just a few, well, like, they were giggling, too. Then it really started. He started this chant thing going. I hate to even repeat it. He kept saying over and over, "Sexy Cobb! Sexy Cobb!" Then he motioned for his moron friends to join in. The idiots did! Only a couple at first, Peter Blake Ward. Like, he needs three names, right? "Sexy Cobb! Sexy Cobb!" I told them to shut up, but that made more of them do it. Finally, almost every boy in the class was chanting. The rest of the girls didn't say anything. They didn't chant, but they didn't tell the boys to shut up. I did, again. Lorraine kept saying, "Stop it, stop it!" But it just got louder. I don't know how the rest of the school didn't hear it.

Finally, Lorraine started to cry, and that made Frank get up from his desk and walk over to her like a hunter, like this (*She demonstrates*), like he's hunting a wild animal. He goes right up to her face, and nose to nose, real nasty, he keeps right on saying it. "Sexy Cobb! Sexy Cobb!" Well, she couldn't take it any more, and she got up and ran out of the room really crying. Frank laughed really loud and started high-fiving his dudes.

Well, Sister Smash You came back and everything was very quiet. She asked Frank where Lorraine was, and he said, very calm, "Like, she went to the bathroom, Sister." Lorraine didn't come back the rest of the day. The next day it all came down. Lorraine had told her parents, and they called Mother Superior—Attila the Nun. When she heard about what happened, she called Frank and his dudes into her office. I think the apology to Lorraine and the letter to her parents was sincere. They don't bother us girls anymore, either. They're still on punishment.

CARMINITA

If it is supposed to be so good here, then why does it hurt?

Please, don't misunderstand. I think that your country is very beautiful, and many of your people are nice. But if I have to go back to that school again in September, I think I will run away back home to Spain. My father says that this is our home now, and I shouldn't think of Spain like that. In my town, my village, all the people know me. Everybody knows my name. I feel like I belong. Like it is . . . never mind. I have a little trouble meeting people because I'm shy and stuff. I was a little lonely and I wanted to make friends, but it is so hard to do that here. The kids in my school have these little groups, clicks, or something, I don't know. Anyway, they'll all be together in little groups in the rec area, talking in little whispers and laughing and pointing at me, like this. (*She demonstrates.*) I just turn and walk away. I just don't seem to fit in. The Mexican girls don't like the way I speak Spanish. They say I have an accent, also, like, they stay *usted*, and I say *tu*, for the word "you." The call me a snob. Not! The white kids call me a Mexican. Not even close.

The thing that hurts is that they call me a lot worse things. I don't even want to be with kids like that. The African-American girls only want help with Spanish vocabulary for class and the boys, well, the ones who look at me, look nice but never say anything. I heard one of the girls say that it means boys are afraid. They're only just boys.

So, I stay home a lot. No use going to the mall, nobody to go with. I have four brothers, so there is no help there. I sometimes watch TV shows from Spain on cable, and that makes me feel all kinds of things— sad, happy, silly. Sometimes, I dance a waltz with King Juan Carlos. It's like this. (*She dances with her imaginary king*) He very nice—tall.

When I grow up, I'd like to have friends who know your name—and can dance.

CAROLYN

Carolyn is finding out that friends come in all shapes and sizes. Sticking together counts a lot.

I guess you probably heard about Maria already. I think she got blamed for stealing the travel money from the school office because she was the last one anybody saw near there. I've known her for, like, forever. I play with her, and she even eats at my house once or twice a week. Her mom works and her father went away, so my mom looks after her, after school on Tuesdays and Wednesdays. That's how we became friends.

All the other girls don't hardly even talk to her. They say that she's a freak on account of her having two-tone skin. She's got some kind of condition that makes her face and arms get these big white splotches. So, like, I really, really care. Yeah, right. What a bunch of freaks they are. Imagine in this day and age, kids being prejudiced like that. It is major lameness! Pog is all they're good for.

So, we were playing in my front yard, and this cop car pulls up. These two big cops get out and say, in these really deep voices, like this (*She imitates them*), "Which one is Marie Oprah Travis?" Marie goes, "That's me, did something happen to my mom at work?" This cop says, "You were seen in the hall outside the school office about the time some money was taken. You have to come with us." Never says a word about Marie's mom. She had to drop a note off from her doctor so she wouldn't have to take P.E. Everybody knows that. Then they put her in the cop car and drove away. I was like shocked.

I told my mom, and she called the school. Then we got in our car and drove over there. I didn't know Mom could drive that fast. When we get there, Marie's mom was already in the office. She and my mom hugged and my mom goes, "We'll straighten this out, don't worry." Then my mom goes to me, "Go sit by Marie and tell her this is going to be all right." I don't know how she knew it, but I sat next to Marie. She was upset but she wasn't afraid. Then my mom told the police how well she knew Marie and would vouch for her. Then—I love this part—she points out the window at all the other kids playing in the playground and goes, "Were any of these other children questioned?" Before the cop answered, the first cop came in and said that he searched Marie's locker and it was clean. I swear, just like some geeky, TV cop. Marie's mom goes, "Who else's locker was searched?" The cop goes, "Nobody, this is the only student mentioned to us." My mom goes to the principal, Mrs. Cochran, "What's going on here, Lucy, any number of people could have taken the money?" The principal, she was, like, speechless. Then mom said the best thing, she goes, "Why don't you check the place where you kept travel money. Marie, do you know where it was kept?" Marie just shook her head from side to side, real slow, like this. (*She demonstrates*)

So, the principal opens a cabinet drawer full of papers and junk, and stuff starts spilling out. It was a mess. Then, Mom, she pushes down on a rod that holds the drawer in the cabinet and pulls it out on to the floor. Bang! Papers fly everywhere. A bigger mess. Stuck behind where the drawer were some envelopes, and a small plastic bag full of money. Case closed.

On the way home, I asked mom how she knew the money was there. She says she didn't, but that she knew Mrs. Cochran back when they where in high school and, "She was disorganized then, and people don't change all that much, they just get older."

It's really cool belonging to this bunch.

BOYS:

RONNY

*I still don't know why or how it happened. I didn't
want this kind of attention. The worst day of my life.*

I know people have these terrible stories about nuns,
but mine is my worst. Here's the thing. I was standing
on line, after lunch, just like everybody. Suddenly,
Sister Agnes grabs my ear and drags me and two other
boys into Sister Patricia's class. Sister Patricia is,
like, the head of the school, or something. Standing in
front of the class, by the blackboard, are like five or
six guys. Her class is laughing and clapping. She tells
Steve, who's standing right next to me, to sing two
songs to the class as punishment. He starts singing
"God Bless America." She says she's heard that song
enough. He says it's the only one he knows, so he
sings it twice. She's furious and smacks him across
the back. Then she tells me to sing two songs for
punishment. I say, "Punishment for what?" She goes
ballistic and hits me, too. I don't want to get hit for
singing "God Bless America," so I start singing this
funny song my soon-to-be brother-in-law taught me
one night before at dinner. My whole family laughed,
so I figure it was cool. It goes like this:
   "I want a beer, just like the beer that pickled dear
old dad.
   It was the beer and the only beer that my dad ever
had.

A real old-fashioned beer, with lots of foam,
It took ten men to carry Daddy home.
I want a beer just like the beer that pickled dear
old dad." [Sung to the tune of "I want a girl, just
like the girl that married dear old dad."]
The class was falling down laughing and clapping
their hands. Two dudes in the first row gave me high-
fives. Sister Patricia grabbed me by the hair and
shoved me against the blackboard, and hit me again.
Then she called this girl over and made her take off
her uniform jacket and tie it around my waist, like a
skirt. Then she got some ribbons from another girl,
and put them in my hair with pins. She rolled up my
pants legs and tied a bow around my neck. I wanted to
die. Everybody that was just laughing *with* me was
now laughing *at* me. Then she tells the oldest girl to
take me around to the other classrooms to sing the
song to them. The first class she took me to was my
class and Sister Ernestine. I started to sing, and the
class started to howl, and Sister Ernestine said, "Sit
down!" She goes to the girl who brought me, "Tell
Sister Patricia that I'll handle it from here."

If I live to be a gazillion years old, I'll always hate
that day. But I still like the song.

RICHARD

Sometimes it happens because people just want a little attention, and sometimes it's an accident.

Jackie Harney hit me in the face with a rock. See this Band-Aid? (*There is a Band-Aid below his left eye*) Jackie threw a rock and hit me. He couldn't ever hit anything with anything his whole life! He's been hanging around us, the gang from the 'hood, not that we're a gang, we're just from . . . we all grew up together. Jackie can't do anything, so he kinda just stands around. He can't hit, catch, kick, throw, or do anything. We were playing touch football in the street, and when we chose up sides, there was one too many guys, and Jackie was that guy. Jackie says, like usual, "Hey, I wanna play. Can't I play?" He can't even play hide-and-seek and get it right. I told him, "If you're seeking, you don't hide!" Anyway, where was I? Oh, yeah, right. So we're playing touch, and getting out of the way of the cars, and Jackie was over on the sidewalk. His job was to say if a car was coming that maybe we didn't see.

We're playing, and Jackie starts throwing rocks into the vacant lot. Sometimes he is so bad at throwing that he can't even hit the lot. After a few plays, a rock lands right near us. The guys started yelling at Jackie to stop throwing rocks over here, and look out for cars. He says okay. A few plays later, I set the ball down to begin a play and as I straighten up, a rock hits me right there—Boom! (*Indicates bandage*) I saw stars, and I went down like this. (*He falls*) The guys all ran over. Ramon ran and phoned my house, and Jackie didn't even know he hit me. Well, I'm bleeding, and Ramon comes back and says nobody is answering at my house. I say, "It's okay, my older brother is an intern at the hospital, call him." They called, and Larry's mom drove us there.

I never saw my brother actually be a doctor before. That was a little cool. He looked at my cut the way a doctor does and nodded, and stuff. (*He demonstrates*) Then he put in stitches. Didn't even hurt. Four stitches. I can't show them to you; germs might get in. He even gave me a shot of something. That didn't hurt, too much, either. Jackie finally remembered to apologize. He's still around, standing off to the side. It's cool, standing is good. It comes to him naturally.

WILLIAM

He always knows where he is and what's going on.
He's now very sure where he belongs.

My father got drunk, and loud, and mean last night. I
didn't know it was going to be like this. I mean, I just
met him a few days ago. I lived with my mother all
my life, and she never talked about him. Sometimes,
when I asked about him, she'd say, "It's a long story
and it's late now, go to bed and we'll talk about it
another time." Another time never came until Mom
was laid off from work. I think that means she lost her
job temporarily.

I came home after school was finally out. Yea! All
summer and no school, a great thing. Mom goes, to
me, she goes, "You're in for a big surprise, you're
going to meet your father. He lives just north of where
you like to go see the otters and sea lions play. Near
the cove you like to fish in. He said he saw you there a
few times from the cliffs."

I never felt so many feelings at one time in my life.
Psych-city, big time! So, we went to his house and
met him. Big dude. His wife was there, and she's cool.
Then Mom drops the other bomb. I'm going to stay
with them for a few weeks. I can call her anytime I
want, just behave myself. She'll see me on the
weekends. Be neat and tidy. She never said "tidy" to
me before in my life.

So, they show me a bedroom and tell me I'll sleep
there. I never had a bedroom before, so this was cool.

Mom kisses me and leaves. I go to bed and start reading, like I always do, and I fall asleep. Next thing I know, I'm awake and there is lots of yelling and a door slams, and then it's quiet. Next day, my father says he's going to work. He goes, "You get in the truck and go with me." Turns out he's some kind of handyman. I stay with him all day. He buys me a tuna sandwich for lunch. I don't help him, I don't get to play, I can't even call Matty, my best friend. We go exploring together in the caves all the time. Used to, anyway.

A couple more days like this: yelling at night, the smell of whiskey, barf time, sitting in a truck all day. Great summer vacation. When I phone, Mom she asks how I am, and I say fine, but it's not true because the night before he got real drunk and he was yelling, and stuff, and then I heard a loud bang. I got out of bed and crawled on my hands and knees to the kitchen where the noise was coming from. When I got there, I saw him grab his wife's hair and pull her down into a chair, real hard. Scared me—you better believe it! Violence is okay in the movies, but not in the kitchen.

So, this morning I called Matty and asked if I could sleep over at his house, and his Mom said it was all right. Then I called Mom and told her what was going on and that Matty's mom said sleeping over was cool. It took me less then five minutes to be gone.

LUCAS

My cousin Artie: a world of his own.

Boy, oh boy! My cousin Artie. He is really something.
He always tells me how great he is and how tough he
is and how he can do all these things, but I never see
him with anybody. I mean, he always comes over to
my house because he doesn't have anyone else to
hang with. He's okay, but I want to pour wet cement
in my ears when he starts that stuff.

First he says words weird. Like he says "lever
mind" when he means never mind . . . and "bueeze"
when he means breeze and "mut" for but. The other
thing he does is that he, like, he invents words all the
time. We were playing cards the other day, he holds
up a seven of clubs and says (*Imitating him*), "I have a
seven of curlies." I didn't know what he was talking
about. I thought he was talking about one of the
Stooges at first. I says, "You mean a seven of clubs."
He says, "Well me and all the dudes I hang with call
them curlies! And these here we call spears." I said,
"Those are spades." He goes, "Well all the dudes I
hang with call them spears. We call them curlies and
spears." I says, "I never saw you play cards with
anybody." He goes to me, "You trying to start
something? Because I beat up a lot of guys and I'm
really tough." I just shut up. I didn't know what to say
to him.

He tells me that all his friends force him to have
fights all the time. Like if they've got a battle, they get

Artie to fight it for them because he's so tough. Well, I never saw him in a fight. I never even heard of him being in a fight. I never heard my aunt say that her son is in fights all the time, and I never met any of these people he talks about. I asked my mother about it, and she said that Artie does get into fights occasionally because he's having a problem dealing with his speech impediment. That thing he does with his *r's* is making him do all that? Too weird, man, I don't even notice it most of the time. Like I don't pay attention to his being fat either. He's just Artie. Sometimes he even makes me laugh. I guess he's a nice guy, but I just don't know when that is.

JAKE

Uncle Sam wants you! Really? Not Leon.

This guy I ride home with on the bus almost every day, Leon, I just don't know about him. I mean, is he Geekie the Geek, or what? I don't know. He always looks for me and tries to sit next to me. That's okay until he starts talking. He always tells me how he can't wait till he gets home from school and gets out of his "civvies" and into his uniform. He calls them his "civvies." He can't wait to put on his Marine uniform. What's up with that? The Marines? I mean, he's just a kid. What would the Marines want with this guy?

Anyway, he seems like he's okay otherwise. We tell jokes and play word games on the bus. Ya know, we play Hang Man or something like that. Everything is fine until he brings up the Marine uniform stuff again. He can't wait to change, blah blah blah. They don't let kids into the Marines. He's still in school. So uncool. So, so what's the point? One day he got up from his seat on the bus and showed me how to march. He was marching up and down the aisle, pretending he had a rifle, and switching it from shoulder to shoulder like this (*He demonstrates close order drill, kind of*): "Right shoulder arms, to the rear, march, left oblique." I thought I was gonna die. People on the bus were cracking up. The bus driver made him sit down, thank God.

One day he gets on the bus and he sits near me while I'm goin' to myself, Don't sit here, don't sit here, don't . . . "Hi!" After a few minutes of not saying anything, he goes, "I won't be changing into my uniform anymore." I go, like I really care, "How come?" He goes, "Because my dad is in the Marines, and he's not going to be married to my mother anymore." "So?" I go. "My parents are divorced. It happens to a lot of kids." He goes. "He's divorcing my mom, and if he's not going to be married to my mother anymore, I don't want to be like him. He's moving to one of the Carolinas. He made her cry. I don't like it when she cries. I'm going home and throw away all my Marine clothes." Then, ya know what he did? He punched the side of the bus. He came over my house later. That's the first time he ever did that.

CASEY

Sometimes the people who are supposed to be helping are the ones who do the most damage.

I was so angry when I came home from school today I didn't want to talk to anybody. It's all Mr. Peabody's fault. I didn't even go outside and play with Georgie, Allan, and Kareem. I didn't watch my favorite shows, and when Mom came home from work, she said I was mumbling under my breath, "I hate him, I hate him," while I was doing my homework. She asked me what was up and I told her, "Peabody!"

Every time I hand in my homework, and there is a small mistake in it, he calls me up to the front of the class and points out the mistake like it's some kind of joke, and the whole class laughs. It happened a couple of times last week. The whole class laughed! He doesn't do it to the other kids. The other teachers tell the class to stop if they laugh at a kid in class, but not Mr. Peabody. I can't even think anymore and I . . . stay off the schoolyard. I'm not giving anyone a chance to laugh at me twice. I don't want to see any of them.

The man has got to die. That's the only answer. I could sneak up on him like this (*He acts it out*) and then jump on him like Batman . . . creeargh! Or maybe I could karate him to death like a Power Ranger! Heeaaa! Hai! (*Doing his best Power Ranger*) I don't watch them; I used to but it's kid stuff now.

I'm going to draw a picture of Mr. Peabody and make it real big. Then I'm going to take it and rip it up in a million pieces, maybe a billion pieces, like this. (*He demonstrates*) Nobody should get laughed at if they make a mistake.

I hope somebody laughs at him when he gets a parking ticket.

AARON

Aaron is going to find out that the more things change, the more they stay the same.

My sister, Gracie, has a new boyfriend, Jerry, and he's pretty cool. He has a car and he can wiggle his left ear. He lives in the next town, so it takes a long time for him to get here, and a long time to get home. He brought me a cool baseball mitt and taught me how to break it in. Gracie used to take me to the park on Saturday afternoon while Mom and Dad worked in the store. Then, after, we'd get strawberry floats. But now she goes somewhere with Jerry. They don't get home until dark and Jerry always says, "I gotta go, I got a long trip." Then Mom winks at Gracie and goes, "Won't you stay for dinner?" He always stays. After dinner, he plays the piano and we sing. He taught me this cool song. It's about (*He sings*), "If you don't give a feather or a fig, you could grow up to be a pig." It's about staying in school, but nice. I sang it to my class, and the teacher threw me out. I guess nuns don't like animals.

Jerry's nice and all, but he talks real loud, especially when Mom and Dad are in the room, but as soon as they leave, he talks real low and whispers in Gracie's ear and then she giggles. If he's saying funny things, he should say them loud enough for everybody to laugh. Why do I have to be left out? I hate being un-included! Sometimes they take me to the movies with them and then we finally have fun.

CARROLL

It's a boy. Let's name him Carroll. A boy named Carroll! Wouldn't wish that on anyone.

Yeah, that's right, my name is Carroll. Don't laugh, Louis Giovanetti laughed and we got into it a little, and we got thrown out of computer lab. I was named after my Uncle Carroll. Ya see, my mother and father named me after him because he's got all the big money in the family. So they kissed up to him and used me as the lips. He's not a bad guy. He's real old and his car is so old that I don't even know what you call it. Akim, the dude who drives him around, says that the old guy sleeps in the back a lot. My Uncle gives me nice presents on my birthday, yeah, right! The guy paid for my tap dance lessons. I didn't want tap dance lessons. It's bad enough being called Carroll. He always wanted to learn how to tap dance when he was my age, but he was afraid his friends would laugh. Look at this! (*He does a little time step. Well or badly, it doesn't matter.*)

When I asked my parents about my name, my father leaves the room. My mom says that a lot of great men have my name. "Carroll O'Conner, the actor, and J. Carroll Naish, the actor, and Carroll Rosenblum, he owned a lot of professional sports teams. There are dozens of others." She really doesn't know any others; she mentions the same three every time.

I tried to come up with a nickname, but nothing caught on. How does Flash sound, or maybe Rockie? I thought about Paul Simon's song (*Sings*) " . . . but you can call me Al, call me Al, naa nanaa na, call me . . . " You know what, though, people would probably think my whole name was Alice. This is so way bad, I . . . I don't know what I'm gonna do. Can't fight for the rest of my life. Remember a boy named Sue? If you come up with a really cool nickname for me, will you let me know right away? Thanks.

ANDRÉ

Camping with Dad, the dog, and the reasons why friends can come in handy.

Don't, unless he's really cool or very lame, go camping with your father.

Here's the deal. My mother left when I was about five. She just said, "Later." She went looking for her singing career, or whatever. So my dad, who's really my foster dad, raised me. He was always kinda broke, so we moved around a lot. So, after we lived in this place we're in now, and I hadn't met anybody to be friends with, like, he decides that, "We'll be buddies, pals. Have a lot of fun together! Yes sirree, Dré. I know . . . we'll go camping!" Oh, man, bonding. We went off to bond. It had come to this okay, so like, we're out in the woods and we're putting up the tent. That was, like, a dance, I swear. First, we bent over and moved in circle to the right, like this, hammering in these metal spikes. (*He demonstrates*) Then we went the other way, like this. (*He demonstrates*) When we finished, not one spike was in straight. I won't even tell you about the tent. If the spikes were a dance, the tent was pure hip-hop. Dad's not good with his hands. I guess my real dad wasn't good either, and he passed it on to me.

Okay, that night we're laying on the ground looking at the stars and he's explaining about which is which and stuff, and then we crawl in the tent and go to sleep. Our German Shepherd plopped right between our sleeping bags. I wake up in the middle of the night, and I look up, and instead of seeing tent I see stars.

So, like, I'm trying to make out if I'm dreaming, or what, and my dog sticks his head out from under the tent, and then a hand reaches out and pulls my sleeping bag back under the tent. Then my father puts the dog outside the tent so he won't drag me and my bag out again, and goes back to sleep. When I wake up in the morning, my dog is chasing jack rabbits and I'm outside the tent again.

This is how pals bond? Nobody even says "pals" anymore.

JAMAL

Whereever you are, it's good to be cool . . . and warm.

It snows here in the winter. Where I come from, it's desert. We moved here because my dad got transferred. I used to like the snow, but I don't much anymore. It's pretty when it's new, but that's it.

Last winter, I got a sled and went out to the hill near here. All the kids from around here go to the hill. I was starting to go on my first run, ya know, I backed up like this (*He demonstrates*), and I'd started to run to the top of the hill, and this big kid stops me. "I go now!" He said. I backed out of the way and start again. I get a good jump and, man, and I'm flying, zoooooommmm! when a guy on another sled crashed into to me and I went flying into a snow bank. I laughed like crazy and pulled myself out of the snow. A little rough but, hey, fun. It happened six more times, and only to me. I was like a target or something.

I stopped going down the hill, and one of them says, "Hey, take another run, we won't bother you." So, duh, I do it again. This time three of them crashed into me. I got up mad, but I couldn't fight them. So I started to leave. I saw them clump together and plan something, so I kept walking, only faster. Then they pushed one of the smaller boys toward me. He comes over and says, "These dudes are so uncool. C'mon, I'll show you a better place. What's your name?" I say, "It's Jamal." He calls to the others, "It's Jamal!"

and as I turned to go, they all ran up and jumped me. They rubbed snow in my face and put it down my neck and back. I couldn't even fight back. I tried to swing at them, but they swarmed over me. Then they all grabbed their sleds and ran away giggling like little girls. One of them kicked my sled. I tried to figure out what I did to them that they should do this. There was no answer. Where I come from this couldn't happen. No snow.

RALPH

*He wanted to belong so badly. Now he doesn't think
he deserves it.*

Where I lived before we moved here was really . . .
better. The kids around here are okay once you . . .
well . . . well . . . when . . . well . . . I don't really know.
I don't really know them. I think it's gonna stay that
way. We moved here right before Labor Day. Boom!
I'm in a new school, I don't know anybody, and I'm a
little bit shy, anyway! Okay? So, finally, I start talking
to Frances Mary, a pretty cool girl who sits behind
me. Took me a week. I said, "Shy." I mean it! So,
then I met some of the cooler guys. Will, Vinnie, Von,
André. But we weren't what you could call tight. So
I'm starting to feel okay about things, and it was kind
of cool, and all so. . . .
   I started walking home the same way as Frances
Mary. Two days later, we're walking together. It's
only eight or ten blocks out of my way. It's cool.
Then, then I was walking her home and, and she had
just told me a joke about . . . about. . . . Well, I can't
say to you what it was, but it was funny. You don't
expect girls to say those things. I think that's what
made it cool. Anyway, a guy is walking toward us
down the hill as we walk up. He had this big dog, not
on a leash. The dog started barking and ran down
toward us and . . . and . . . and ya know what I did? I
could have done a lot of things, like stand still, or get
between Frances Mary and the dog, lots of things. But

. . . but, like, the king of creepy dweebs, I ducked behind Frances Mary! I can't believe it! I'm dead! The dog didn't do anything. He just ran down the hill! I was . . . I was . . . I just ran home!

I sit right in front of her in class. AAAAAAAA! I'm dead! Dead!

GERALD

"Let's go hiking. Hiking is so cool." Yeah, right.

Me on a hike, with Otto and Keeko? Too much, man. I couldn't believe it. I was sitting on my porch and they came by and said, "We're going hiking, wanna come?" Me? They never even ever look at me. So, I go, "Cool." Otto, Keeko, and me? Too much. So, we hike on a path through the woods heading for the swampy area. I was last, and then I was in front. Okay, right? Cool. We come to the pond, and as usual, the banks were way muddy. Over off to the side was a used-to-be fire still smoking. Near that was a kind of a raft. Someone had just been there. So, we get on the raft, and with big sticks for poles, we pushed out on the pond. Okkaayyyy! It's way cool!

We get to the other side of the pond, and where it's not too much mud near the bank, the two big guys jump off and land on a not-too-muddy spot. I can't jump that far. I'm stuck on the raft, holding onto the pole. (*He demonstrates*) The raft and the pole were going in two different directions. Like this. (*He demonstrates*) Otto and Keeko started laughing, and I had to decide to either let go of the pole or let go of the raft. Duh! A real no-brainer. I hung onto the pole. The raft went away and I landed in the water. No duh! I managed to get the nearly dead fire going and dried my clothes some, so I wouldn't get in trouble when I got home. The other guys vaporized. Hiking sucks.

ROGER

Sometimes you just don't know what to do even if you do know who to ask.

There are these guys on my block. They're all pretty cool. I tried to . . . you know . . . join them, and be friendly, and associate with them. In my opinion, that would have been good for me. So, one day, I engaged them in conversation. I even used words they like. Like "cool" and "like" and others . . . I've forgotten. During our verbal exchange, I found them to be fun-loving and friendly. They often punched each other in the arm and giggled, but I didn't mind. They said if I wanted to hang out with them that I had to skateboard. I don't skateboard. "Well," they said, "how about rollerblading?" I said, "I ride horses and I like astronomy." They thought that was very funny. They asked me to get on a skateboard. I reluctantly did. I tried to balance myself as I rolled (*He demonstrates*) forward, but I lost my balance and fell, like this. (*He demonstrates*) They all laughed again. I guess I'm funnier than I thought.

I went home, sore, and tried to think of things that would make them like me. I talked about it with Cliff when we went riding with Manuel. They didn't have any answers. I talked it over with Morris, Angela, and Cynthia in my astronomy club. Nothing. My sister said, "Learn to dance." Then she offered to teach me. Nobody had any real answers. I was very perplexed.

Well, I'm going to ask my mother to buy me some clothes that are several sizes too large and try to remember those words those boys use. I would like to have friends to share my recreation time. Otherwise, what have I got?

BRUNO

He seems to like himself just as he is.

Okay! Let's get one thing straight before we even start! I am not fat! Okay, I carry a lot of weight around, but I'm not uncomfortable with it. Everybody else seems to have a problem with it but me. Like, I went out for the basketball team and the coach looked at me like I had a disease, or something. The other kids started making fun of me during the lay-up drills. The coach starts giving people things to do to see how good they are; he doesn't even look at me. I noticed that when the other kids where dribbling the ball that they were all looking at the ball! Finally, after everybody else, he goes to me, "Now, son, what's your name? Oh, yeah, Finelli, here's how to bounce the ball. You put your hand up here. . . . " He called me "Son." What a geekmeister! I'm thinking this guy is a major spaz, and I take the ball to the end line and take it out. Just stopped listening to the phlegm-brain. I move it up the court nice and easy, like this (*He demonstrates*), and I'm looking everywhere but at the ball. I see a guy cut to the basket and I hit him with a pass. It surprises him a little, but he catches it and he scores way easy. Everybody stops and stares at me except the guy I hit with the pass—he gives me a high-five. The coach goes, "Son, run that once more." Again with the "Son" business. We run the set again, and this time I hit him with a bounce pass. Another basket. I do it three or four more times—basket every time. The defense was even looking for it and we scored anyway. Then they're all congratulating the guy who made the baskets and nobody is saying anything to me!

After practice, they're all high-fiving each other and talking about going for pizza . . . nobody says anything to me. Zilch, zero, nada. Then old Spaz comes up to me and says, "Nice going, Finelli, can you dribble with your left hand, too?" I said, "Sure." As I was walking off the court, I heard him say, "The fat boy's really good."

At least he stopped calling me "Son."

ORDER DIRECT

MONOLOGUES THEY HAVEN'T HEARD, Karshner. Speeches for men and women. $8.95.
MORE MONOLOGUES HAVEN'T HEARD, Karshner. More living-language speeches. $8.95.
SCENES THEY HAVEN'T SEEN, Karshner. Modern scenes for men and women. $8.95.
FOR WOMEN: MONOLOGUES THEY HAVEN'T HEARD, Pomerance. $8.95.
MONOLOGUES for KIDS, Roddy. 28 wonderful speeches for boys and girls. $8.95.
MORE MONOLOGUES for KIDS, Roddy. More great speeches for boys and girls. $8.95.
SCENES for KIDS, Roddy. 30 scenes for girls and boys. $8.95.
MONOLOGUES for TEENAGERS, Karshner. Contemporary teen speeches. $8.95.
SCENES for TEENAGERS, Karshner. Scenes for today's teen boys and girls. $7.95.
HIGH-SCHOOL MONOLOGUES THEY HAVEN'T HEARD, Karshner. $8.95.
MONOLOGUES from the CLASSICS, ed. Karshner. $8.95.
SHAKESPEARE'S MONOLOGUES THEY HAVEN'T HEARD, ed. Dotterer.$8.95.
MONOLOGUES from CHEKHOV, trans. Cartwright. $8.95.
MONOLOGUES from GEORGE BERNARD SHAW, ed. Michaels. $7.95.
MONOLOGUES from OSCAR WILDE, ed. Michaels. $7.95.
WOMAN, Pomerance. Monologues for actresses. $8.95.
MODERN SCENES for WOMEN, Pomerance. Scenes for today's actresses. $7.95.
MONOLOGUES from MOLIERE, trans. Dotterer. $9.95.
SHAKESPEARE'S MONOLOGUES for WOMEN, ed. Dotterer. $8.95.
DIALECT MONOLOGUES, Karshner/Stern.13 essential dialects applied to contemporary monologues. Book and cassette tape. $19.95.
YOU SAID a MOUTHFUL, Karshner. Tongue twisters galore. $8.95.
TEENAGE MOUTH, Karshner. Modern monologues for young men and women. $8.95.
SHAKESPEARE'S LADIES, ed. Dotterer. $7.95.
BETH HENLEY: MONOLOGUES for WOMEN, Henley.*Crimes of the Heart*, others. $8.95.
CITY WOMEN, Smith. 20 powerful, urban monologues. Great audition pieces. $7.95.
KIDS' STUFF, Roddy. 30 great audition pieces for children. $8.95.
KNAVES, KNIGHTS, and KINGS, ed. Dotterer. Shakespeare's speeches for men. $8.95.
DIALECT MONOLOUES, VOL II, Karshner/Stern. 14 more important dialects. Farsi, Afrikaans, Asian Indian, etc. Book and cassette tape. $19.95.
RED LICORICE, Tippit. 31 great scene-monologues for preteens. $8.95.
MODERN MONOLOGUES for MODERN KIDS, Mauro. $8.95.
A WOMAN SPEAKS: WOMEN FAMOUS, INFAMOUS and UNKNOWN, ed.Cosentino. $9.95.
FITTING IN. Monologues for kids, Mauro. $8.95.
VOICES. Speeches from writings of famous women, ed. Cosentino. $9.95.
FOR WOMEN: MORE MONOS THEY HAVEN'T HEARD, Pomerance. $8.95.
NEIL SIMON MONOLOGUES. From the plays of America's foremost playwright. $12.95.
CLASSIC MOUTH, ed. Cosentino. Speeches for kids from famous literature. $8.95.
POCKET MONOLOGUES for WOMEN, Pomerance. 30 modern speeches. $8.95.
WHEN KIDS ACHIEVE, Mauro. Positive monologues for preteen boys and girls. $8.95.
FOR WOMEN: POCKET MONOLOGUES from SHAKESPEARE, Dotterer. $8.95
MONOLOGUES for TEENAGE GIRLS, Pomerance. $8.95.
POCKET MONOLOGUES for MEN, Karshner. $8.95.
COLD READING and HOW to BE GOOD at IT. Hoffman. $9.95.
POCKET MONOLOGUES: WORKING-CLASS CHARACTERS FOR WOMEN. Pomerance. $8.95.